Love Letters
To My Daughters-in-Law

Love Letters
To My Daughters-in-Law

Cathy Edgett

Heart Happy
Mill Valley California

Love Letters to my Daughters-in-Law
Copyright © 2014 Cathy Edgett. All rights reserved. Printed in the United States of America. No part of this book may be used or reproduced in any manner without prior written permission, except in the case of brief quotations embodied in critical articles and reviews.

    Cover Photo: Cathy Edgett
    Interior/cover design by JM Shubin, ShubinDesign

    CATALOGING DATA:
    Love Letters to my Daughters-in-Law
    By Cathy Edgett
    Memoir

    ISBN: 978-0-9916174-0-1

Dedicated to the wise woman within us all

How does it feel to be at peace and fully awake?
You could be like this in perfect quiet
　　And you could be like this in the wildest dance.
　　It's your birthright!

　　　　　　　　—Charlotte Selver
　　　　　　　　Every Moment is a Moment

Table of Contents

Part 1: Rewriting the Myth
- Letter One: A Probe — 17
- Letter Two: Brewing Our Own Myth — 19
- Letter Three: The Cauldron — 21
- Letter Four: Emptying and Filling — 23
- Letter Five: Heart is the Hook — 25

Part 2: Moving Into Intimacy
- Letter Six: This Moment — 29
- Letter Seven: The Umbilical Cord — 30
- Letter Eight: Exploring the Well — 32
- Letter Nine: Gratitude's Fuel — 34
- Letter Ten: Two Sides Made One — 36

Part 3: Expansion
- Letter Eleven: Return — 41
- Letter Twelve: Listening Touch — 43
- Letter Thirteen: Beginner's Mind — 45
- Letter Fourteen: Casting — 47
- Letter Fifteen: Giving Time — 49

Part 4: Knowing, Tradition, Release
- Letter Sixteen: Solitude — 52
- Letter Seventeen: Tradition — 54
- Letter Eighteen: Tradition Re-Mixed — 56
- Letter Nineteen: Perfection Release — 58
- Letter Twenty: Perfection Reframed — 60

Part 5: Today's Curve of the Tribe
    Letter Twenty-One: Women Today   64
    Letter Twenty-Two: Such Wealth   67
    Letter Twenty-Three: Play with Blocks   69
    Letter Twenty-Four: Acceptance   71
    Letter Twenty-Five: Value of the Tribe   73

Part 6: Artistry
    Letter Twenty-Six: Lifting the Veil   76
    Letter Twenty-Seven: Authenticity   78
    Letter Twenty-Eight: One of My Ways   80
    Letter Twenty-Nine: Art of Love   83
    Letter Thirty: Life as Hour-glass   85

Part 7: A Caress You Inspire
    Letter Thirty-One: Donkey-Time   88
    Letter Thirty-Two: Pain   90
    Letter Thirty-Three: Forgiveness   92
    Letter Thirty-Four: Permission   94
    Letter Thirty-Five: Communion   96

Part 8: Threshold
    Letter Thirty-Six: Receiving   100
    Letter Thirty-Seven: A Moving View   102
    Letter Thirty-Eight: Answer the Request   104
    Letter Thirty-Nine: Conclusion as Threshold 106
    Letter Forty: Bringing in My Sons   108

Dedicated to My Daughters-in-Law and Their Husbands, My Sons:

I wrote this book because I trust the love and care of my two daughters-in-love. I meant to type daughters-in-law, but I am already changed by beginning to write these words. These two women are my daughters-in-love. Their example allows me to speak, to find my voice. I was raised on the cusp of change. I look at them, and see what I might have been, if I had been born when they were born. I continue to learn from my sons, and now, in addition, I learn from these two women, these two precious and inspiring gifts. They widen and expand my view.

I am grateful that without the pain of labor, I gained a daughter, and then, a year later, another. I am graced with two. I now understand how my mother-in-law felt about me, why she loved me so much. This book began as an invitation to ritual. I wanted my daughters-in-law and me to state, either privately, or in front of friends, that we, too, were committed to something bigger than ourselves. Perhaps the ritual could be a walk, a lunch in the park, or a larger announcement that we, too, unite.

The idea for these letters began when my oldest son married. Though I had known his wife since she was fourteen, and we had a relationship of our own, I understood that with the marriage a shift had taken place. She was now first, and that was how it should be. There was also relief. She was responsible for my son, and he, for her. Of course, I was also now responsible for her, and she, for me. We united in those formidable words, *in law*.

My sense is that the words in this book could only be written by a woman who did not have a daughter of her own, and yet, that may not be true. My mother-in-law birthed a daughter, and yet she was clear that I was special too. I loved her son. We shared a bond, a bond of discernment and good taste.

I sensed though some friction for my own mother around that bond. Perhaps it was insecurity or awareness that there is only so much time, and she wanted to spend as much of that time as possible with me. I also wanted to spend time with her. She was my best friend, and I knew her womb, and through that beginning, a structure for my life. Now, with time to reflect, I realize I might have known my mother-in-law more fully if I hadn't been so aware of my own mother and her needs. On the other hand, I know my mother-in-law through her son. I know enough.

I began these letters with a desire for ceremony and ritual. I came to see that I was healing what was past. I was offering a link to my mother-in-law, to my mother, and to all who came before.

For me, life is like a kaleidoscope, confined within boundaries and parameters, and yet changing over and over again. My daughters-in-love bring new colors and shapes to my kaleidoscope, new patterns, and most of all they give to me and my kaleidoscope, inspiration, joy, comfort, warmth, and new ways of perceiving the changing circles of light.

I am grateful. I dedicate this book specifically to two women, Jan and Frieda, and to two men, Jeff and Chris, as well as to the wise woman within us all.

Preface

With my sons grown and married, I enjoy a new kind of freedom. I have time to explore and play with curiosity. I wonder why there are so many mother-in-law jokes. I cringe. What other group is still so attacked without censure?

I understand that historically, and even today, the relationship has not been an invitation to friendship and understanding. In some cultures, the daughter-in-law was handed to the mother-in-law as servant or slave. She was property and pawn. This still occurs, but I'm not talking about that. I'm talking about two women who love one man, a man known differently by each. I also recognize that two women may marry each other, or likewise two men. The question is, "How do families combine?"

Unfortunately, sometimes, not well, and yet this bond forged in ancestral caves, began when family connections were essential for survival of the tribe. We share rings, rings of a family tree, now grafted as two become one.

Inspired by the words of Jelaluddin Rumi, "What nine months does for the embryo, forty early mornings will do for your growing awareness," I present forty letters. There is fragility in these letters, impermanence. I toss them to you, knowing ripples form and spread.

Living as Kaleidoscope

Pick up a twig, extension,
a limb alive in your hand,
connected to heart, liver, lungs, and gut.

Draw a circle; fill it with pews,
add doors like wings,
windows stained, wounds

Breathe a roundness so full,
the place where the cord once attached,
opens inside out

light travels in roles:
Girl – Woman – Crone,
each part joined, with wisdom, at the heart.

—Cathy

Part 1:
Rewriting the Myth

Letter One:
A Probe

To You I Love,

We no longer marry with the illusion of a fairy tale ending, "And they lived happily ever after." We know there is work to be done, work around listening and compromise, forgiveness and acceptance. Resilience is a given, as we share laughter and tears, and yet, though the husband and wife relationship has evolved, the image of the mother-in-law and daughter-in-law relationship has not. It is the subject of jokes, jokes I didn't feel until I became a mother-in-law. Then, I felt hurt, embarrassed. Since humor often covers pain, I wondered what was going on. How had the mother-in-law escaped the mantle of respect and political correctness? Maybe mother-in-laws really are difficult, but I don't like labels, and I don't like being lumped into a group, especially in a negative way.

    I think now of fairy tales like *Snow White*, where a jealous stepmother won't let go of a false illusion of beauty, and uses wiles and witchcraft to destroy the youth, beauty, and innocence of another. Why would we give this image, this story of an older woman poisoning a younger one to our children, to our little girls? We survive as a species because we nurture, support, and protect our young. Elders are meant to offer wisdom and sacrifice, not poison.

"But that's a stepmother," you say, and yet in researching this, I was surprised to learn that an early use of the word mother-in-law, in addition to "mother of one's spouse," was "stepmother". The Brothers Grimm wrote about the evil stepmother. They also wrote a fragmentary fairy tale, *The Evil Mother-in-Law*, and placed it in the first edition of their tales. These tales do not create harmony, nor do they honor natural process, seasons, acceptance, non-judgment, and cycles of change. They don't honor the passage we travel, the wrinkles we earn.

My aim with this letter, and those that follow, is to cleanse the mother-in-law and daughter-in-law relationship with a sweep of the broom that once defined the witch. I want to re-write the simplistic fairy tale world of black and white, good and evil. I want to bring the Wise Woman forward, and bring her back. I honor that every woman is wise, wise when young, wise with age.

I intend to end the poison apple tale with a quest, feminine in nature, to celebrate renewal, birth, and a beauty that emerges and transforms with age and death. We share a journey, you and I, where streams divide, and streams unite. We can vow to honor all stages of the feminine: maiden, woman, and crone. The masculine, too, is given a place. We are one, and we are strong.

Willing the way to begin,
Cathy, a comfortably cozy, wise woman crone

Letter Two:
Brewing Our Own Myth

To You I Love,

We live in an age where we are given the opportunity to brew our own myth. In the past, we had two choices, fight or flight. Now, we can learn to reprogram ourselves, to give ourselves time, when appropriate, before we run, hide, or attack. We may have been raised on the theory of survival of the fittest. Now, we look around and see interdependence.

I was raised on the words, "Sticks and stones may break my bones, but words can never hurt me." Now, I know that isn't true. Words hurt, and not speaking hurts too.

In 1948, Pearl Buck wrote in *Pavilion of Women* about a mother-in-law who saw the value of the legacy her daughters-in-law would nurture and carry on. She supported and educated them. We see the love between Naomi and Ruth in the Bible. These are positive examples of the relationship, but Lisa See in her novel *Dreams of Joy*, about China in the late 1950's writes of a mother who whispers on her daughter's wedding night, *"Always show the greatest kindness to the ones you like the least. If you show kindness to your mother-in-law, who like all women has been bred to hate her daughter-in-law, then you will create an obligation she will never be able to repay."* Can you imagine beginning marriage with those words? It's time to brew a new myth. We can each be our own fairy godmother. We can each wave a wand that celebrates diversity, heals and unifies the past, and welcomes what comes.

We still say the sun rises and sets, yet we know it is the earth that turns. What turns in each of us as we dance in the light of our own moon, waving our own wand, brewing the stories that feed our truth? What turns, and in that turning, renews?

Continually brewing my own myth,
Cathy, sowing transformation with celebration and play

Letter Three:
The Cauldron

To You I Love,

As a child, I had a recurring dream. In the dream, I stood outside the entry to my home looking through the picture window at a huge, black cauldron. A witch dressed in black with a pointed hat presided over a steaming brew. I would wake from the dream terrified. I didn't understand the dream as a child, and yet though the witch was frightening, I often chose to be a witch for Halloween, and I always saw myself as "good" even when wearing a black coned hat and carrying a broom. I think now we inherit a history that demonizes and fears the power of the witch, because she is the third stage of the female. She is crone, healer, wise woman, connected to nature, and seasonal cycles. She gathers, dries, and cures with plants and herbs. I see now the childhood dream, as an omen, a premonition of the woman I would become. I've come to know we women each have a cauldron, a beautiful inner space, a womb, and we choose what to offer, stir, nourish, and brew.

    The ancestral cauldron may be old, formed of iron and memory from the past, but what we place inside is new, is ours to choose. Let's choose with care. There is no poison apple and nothing to fear when we brew what brings forth the tasks that fuel and nourish the fulfillment of our quest.

> *When I open the apple within,*
> *the seeds of my heart*
> *spill forth in trees,*
> *well-fueled,*
> *with roots, branches*
> *and pollinating bees.*

Keeping the fire under my cauldron burning,
Cathy, who evolves in circles like rings in trees

Letter Four:
Emptying and Filling

To You I Love,

A friend asks, "How does a daughter-in-law have enough self-confidence and trust to witness and honor the love between mother and son without it triggering her own inadequacies? How do mother-in-law and daughter-in-law not get into an unconscious competition over the care of one man, who is husband and son?" How indeed? Why are we here but to learn exactly this? We are here to explore. Curiosity is our wand, and we each have our cauldron in which to brew a personal stew.

    I became interested in this subject many years ago, when I was a young mother. A friend was angry when her mother-in-law came to visit and got up early to make muffins, or some other breakfast treat. My friend was convinced her mother-in-law wanted to make her look bad. I, who love to rise early and bake, thought maybe said mother-in-law just liked to bake, or maybe she wanted to give, and baking was how she showed gratitude for an invitation into this home. I saw that I might have risen and baked, with no intention to replace, denigrate, or offend. It was my first inkling of the complexity of the mother-in-law and daughter-in-law relationship. It's been with me ever since. It has also allowed me to understand that mother-in-law may see family, and daughter-in-law may see guest.

Recently I woke from a dream where I was searching for crown jewels. In the dream, I held a tiny box shaped like a house in my hand, certain it contained the jewels for which I searched, but when I opened it, it was empty. Where were the jewels? Then, I realized the emptiness was the jewels. I was given space, space to allow something new and magnificent to enter, space to cultivate, nourish, and fill. What is more crown jewel, more valuable, than that?

Women know the pull of the tides. The menstrual cycle, phased to the moon, allows us to empty and fill. We know fullness and release, passage and wealth.

> In honor of the journey's tides,
> *Cathy*, who basks in the light of the moon

Letter Five:
Heart is the Hook

To You I Love,

Have I said it enough? I am grateful for you. I bow and curtsy in gratitude for you.

Now might I make a request? It can be our first ritual, our first celebration.

Can we stand and denounce these words: *"Mirror, Mirror, on the wall, who's the fairest of them all?"*

We might say instead:

"Mirror, mirror on the wall, the dark, dangerous wall of judgment and comparison, be gone! Be banished from the kingdom, the kingdom of ourselves, a round, roomy, welcoming kingdom of abundance, appreciation, compassion, non-judgment and self-esteem!"

And perhaps we could say:

"I wake myself with a wand, a personal wand, a wand sparkling with the true meaning of what is fair. Kindness is what I see when I look in the mirror. Kindness brewed in the cauldron, a cauldron, rich and full, abundant and overflowing with the bounty of generosity, gratitude, and heart."

You might ask, *"Why kindness out of all the many qualities to value?"* There are two reasons. First, in fourth grade I was the fairy godmother who gave the gift of *kindness* in the play *Sleeping Beauty*. I bring that memory back and polish it like glass. The second, more important reason comes from years ago when I participated in a workshop, a three month commitment called *Eyes of the Beholder*. We learned that when we view ourselves more kindly, we view the world more kindly.

We looked in the mirror, literally looked in the mirror, and the longer we looked, the more kindly we saw, and then when we went out into the world, we realized that others interacted with us in a whole new way. It became clear to each of us that not only do we create the lens through which we look, but the lens we create affects how others see us. In *Eyes of the Beholder*, we were given a wand to wave and change the world, no magic needed at all.

I know now that when I see with love, I am seen with love. The heart is the hook on which to hang the mirror in which we look. The heart is the hook.

>Joyfully cleansing my lens,
>*Cathy*, who rounds her wand on gentle curves

Part 2:
Moving into Intimacy

Letter Six:
This Moment

To You I Love,

When His Holiness, the Dalai Lama, was asked to reveal the happiest moment of his life, he paused, thought, and answered, "I think ... Now!"

I like that.

It takes competition out of the line-up of moments, and competition unwisely utilized is not our friend.

How many times in a day are we asked, "What was the best ....?"

I heard Pam Houston speak about telling a friend that her book was on the New York Times Best Seller list. The response was, "What number?" She knew the next question would be "How many weeks?" It's a game we cannot win.

Therefore, I suggest we put comparison to rest, which is not to say I don't understand choice and discernment.

What is the happiest moment of my life?

I think ... Now!

Now!

Now!

     Honoring a moment well-received,
     Cathy, embracing intimacy, now

Letter Seven:
The Umbilical Cord

To You I Love,

I walk outside and my eye is caught on a line of spider silk shining in the early morning light. Stretching from a branch of the alder tree to an eave on the roof of the house, it is thick and wet with fog.

My husband and I have been discussing the umbilical cord. He says as much as he loves our sons, and he does, he can't imagine that actual physical connection, that physical cord, that nine month presence in the womb.

And the cord is cut, and it is cut again, when the child sits, walks, talks, goes to school, kindergarten, high school, possibly, college, and then, it is deeply and generously cut, deeply and generously transformed, with the son's commitment to another.

We rejoice in that cut, that transformation, and the vow that joins.

And yet for both bride and groom, there is a line of connection with that motherly womb that lit by an inner eye, curves the years like a nautilus shell. For those who are adopted, there is a celebratory spiral as two or more mothers twine. There is an ancestral connection for us all. We all know Mother Earth.

When I trekked in Nepal, I traveled with a young Nepalese man, Sonam, and I saw how connected he was to the people in his village. He also connected to us, to those with whom he traveled. We mattered to him. He sent me a poem, entreating me to return.

> *Mountain can't fly, neither can I, you must come;*
> *you must try.*

I probably won't return to Nepal, but the cords are there, like the lines of a spider's web we don't always see, except in certain light. But just as we hold the line of a jump rope with another, we hold memories, and swing them like garlands. Like the strings in a hammock when we enter, there's a bend.

I can't replace your mother, and I wouldn't want to, but I do want to create a niche, a place to be. I want to honor that we, too share a cord. Perhaps these words are enough. They are enough for me. And, of course, I honor your needs and niche, your point of view on connection and cords.

> Honoring the cords of my life,
> *Cathy*, in love with hammocks, garlands, and swings

Letter Eight:
Exploring the Well

To You I Love,

I don't believe that curiosity killed the cat because I have two wonderfully curious cats and they are snuggly and cuddly, and they love to stick their sweet pink noses in all sorts of places and claw, knead, and explore. They also love to sleep.

I think curiosity is a deep well, a well full of water and stones, each stone with a story. We can hold a stone in our hand, turn it over, and know there is something to learn if we listen, listen within.

When I hold a stone in my hand, I try to listen and feel where this stone has been. Sometimes I see the caves of Lascaux and imagine something written there, something painted or drawn. Other times, I make a wish upon a stone. I wish upon it as if it were a star.

I understand it may or may not be easy to get a story from a stone, but what about those around us. Do we listen? Ask?

I wish I'd asked more questions of those I love who've passed. I wish I'd listened, not as duty, but as prayer.

I'm asking now. Do you have something you want or need to share?

No pressure.

The well is deep, and full of listening stones.

Some stones may be like stars and others may be galaxies. How do we know what reigns within a stone? How do we know what sparks in each of us?

You and I have time to pull the light like taffy, to celebrate density and space. We rise and fall, empty and fill, speak and listen, sing and dance. We can be silent; we can be still. We can touch with the density of stone, and radiate like stars.

> With reverence for touch,
> *Cathy,* honoring light and dark

Letter Nine:
Gratitude's Fuel

To You I Love,

The relationship between mother and son is archetypal. He learns about love in her womb. She learns about love as she carries him, and as he births. The cord is cut many times. The journey has steps.

When the son is young, he wants to marry his mother. He brings her flowers, and makes hearts for her from paper, clay, and blocks. She is his, for a time, and then, he outgrows her, and she adjusts, and this happens over and over again. The relationship reflects the seasons, the movement of streams into rivers, and rivers into seas, the release of leaves, and the flowering that leads to fruit.

The earth renews.

That tender spot where the cord is cut rests, memory dappled as a fawn, as the mother sees her son grow into a man, a man who needs a woman, a man who needs you.

This is where we bond, you and I, in gratitude and trust.

I give thanks to your mother for the day you were born.

I am grateful she carried and nurtured you. I give thanks for cords cut and re-formed, like waves of sand on the beach.
   I give thanks, and there, is fuel.

>   Replete with gratitude,
>   *Cathy,* a woman in love with waves and sand

Letter Ten:

Two Sides Made One

To You I Love,

I have been a daughter-in-law and now I am a mother-in-law. I know what it is to enter a man's life and cling to the illusion that I am the only one, was ever the only one. I also know what it is to release my sons to another, to know the days when I was their "only one" are over, or perhaps, absorbed into an even greater growth and expansion. My sons were, and are, my greatest teachers. What greater gift, what greater reward, than for me to know I prepared my sons to love a woman, and love her generously and well.

I know now that my mother-in-law saw how much her son needed me. She appreciated me, was grateful to me. She handed him over with gratitude. "Here, I've done what I can. He's yours."

I'm grateful to you. I've done what I can. I offer these words of Lao Tzu: *Being deeply loved by someone gives you strength, while loving someone deeply gives you courage.*

I think this business of living is a Mobius strip. Though it may seem as though there are two sides, your side and another, a top and a bottom, a front and a back, there's only one side. With intention, we move along that one side as it curves and twists. The snail secretes a trail of mucous that allows it to glide over the blade of a razor with ease. We, too, can leave a trail, a trail that allows us to curve earth and sky, fairy tale and modern life. We know how to do, and we know how to be. We give and receive, knowing that the two sides of the coin of the realm are really one.

We meet with stickiness as our slide.

>Blessed Be,
>*Cathy*, who glides in and out of her shell

Part 3:
Expansion

Letter Eleven:
Return

To You I Love,

"Wait a minute," you say, "What is this about a hand-off?"

Why do I seem happy to get him off my hands? I'm not happy to "unload" him, but I do understand natural processes, cycles, seasons. I want what is best for my son. Clearly that is you. Together the two of you create something new. I'm curious to see what blossoms and blooms.

My world forms around my love of trees. I love to sit next to trees and envision their rings. I imagine myself growing old by adding rings, and that is how I grow. You are a ring, and your family is too. You are part of my widening circles, my growth and expansion, tree to forest, root to sky.

One house I lived in as a child had a tree that anchored one side of our yard. I can't say what kind of tree it was, but I could climb up and in, and stand and sit in a center that opened out like a flower giving me a place to nest. Branches rose above me. I was embraced 360 degrees around. There is no front or back to a tree. Held by a tree, I, too, breathed 360 degrees around.

With the birth of my sons, my focus cradled in on them. I bent to protect, and my ever-expanding womb focused attention in front. The path was ahead. Goals were set. The birth of responsibility broadened my shoulders, spread my feet. I would protect my sons no matter what. The mother bear had nothing on me. I could be fierce.

    With the marriage of my sons, I again return to that place of embrace, that childhood tree. Blood stirs in a circulatory system without leaks. I bleed no more. Menstrual cycles are done. I know the young girl, the woman, the crone. I am centered, like a tree, and, in that, I offer roots, and branches from which to swing. I offer shade. I offer the brace of my heart.

> Enjoying movement of water and sap,
> *Cathy*, who knows embrace

Letter Twelve:
Listening Touch

To You I Love,

Again, I return to trees. I live where it is quiet. I dissect the silence. How much reverberates in me? When am I touched? Do I hear worms open and recast the soil, snakes glide, squirrels shake the trees? Do I feel and anchor the movement of wings?

One day, a redwood tree leaned toward me. It was about four feet tall, grown from a six inch sprout given to us as we left a day at Scout-a-Rama. I was sitting on the front step crying, and the tree leaned a branch over and in, and stroked my back. It is something to be comforted by a tree, something to remember, and yet, that obvious a movement, I've noticed only once, which may be my fault since there they stand, waiting for us to sit and ask.

Though we don't think trees talk, sometimes the wind makes it seem they do. We, too, play with wind. We use our tongue like a rudder, and harness our breath with words like sails. Do we notice the movement of air? Sometimes, we do.

I try to be sensitive to the wind and soil, earth, and sky, and yet, I wonder, "Am I sensitive to you?" Can you tell me when I'm not?

Where I live the fog can be a glove to the ground. The embrace is moist, and I feel like a blade of grass flowered with dew.

And then there is sun.

My intention is to open to you, to notice and honor change and mood, to come to you and touch, where dew meets sun, trees lean, and the wings of birds are fans for leaves.

> Listening,
> *Cathy,* moistening to receive

Letter Fourteen:
Casting

To You I Love,

Years ago, I crawled through the Tactile Dome at the Exploratorium in San Francisco. It was dark and cramped, and at first, I was afraid. Then, I began to settle into myself, and to enjoy maneuvering by feel. I tunneled through velvet, wool, silk, sand, stone, and grit, climbing up, and sliding down. I'm not suggesting we are Tactile Domes, but I want to uncover ways to know you, ways that aren't invasive, but instead like the touch of a newly mown lawn, with its offer of scent and maybe a nap. I also want to know you like the leaf knows the sun, actively. Can we roam like water striders, hop like bugs, untangle like millipedes, and spiral like the shells of snails?

With age, or should I say maturity, I find myself desiring flexibility and agility. I want a mobile spine. When my mother was nineteen, she watched her father die. Part of his transition was heartbreak. He couldn't accept that WWI, the War to End All Wars, did not, but instead resulted in WWII. His son would leave, would go to Europe to fight. He could not bend for that. My mother watched, and determined she would bend, not break. She would become the willow tree. That was her way to meet what comes, and that worked for her, but I, watching her, chose a firmer stance, until, now, after her death, I soften, and beckon the dissolve of ash.

At a crafts fair I was entranced with a necklace that was cast in silver from the dried inner layer of a prickly cactus. What I saw was a labyrinth formed from the workings of a well-defended plant. I found myself wanting to cast and recast my need for boundary, for light, and shade. Now, as recognition of that, I talk to my vertebrae. I invite each one to separate from the other, and be its own float in a spinal parade.

Women used to meet with wreaths on their heads and dance in the light of the moon. That may be more than we are prepared for, so I suggest we meet in our own creation and cast of ritual. Perhaps, we meet, each as Queen Bee, each in full support of her hive, each open to permeability and shelter, and the guiding light inside.

    Casting the light,
    Cathy, entranced with uniting in and out

Letter Fifteen:
Giving Time

To You I Love,

Georgia O'Keefe wrote, "Nobody sees a flower really; it is so small. We haven't time, and to see takes time—like to have a friend takes time."

To have a friend takes time, perhaps gives time, as we now speak of caregivers rather than caretakers. I wonder if we can plan a play-date, you and I. I know your time is valuable, as is mine, and yet wouldn't it be fun to be snow globes together, shaken, or not.

I come now to the question of which came first, the chicken or the egg.

There is a place of dissolution in the cocoon, where the caterpillar is gone, and the butterfly not yet formed. How is it then with the chicken and the egg? Do they form at the same time? Do you and I? Can we be separated? Would we want to be separated? Well, yes, maybe, occasionally, and, yes, more than that, and yet we know interconnection. We know we are dependent on one another, that sometimes I am leaf, and you are lung, and vice versa. We share in play, no matter what.

Today I treat time like a cat,
asleep on a bed, purring,
with dreams of wings and paw-sifted air,
lovingly creamed with connection and care.

Content to pause,
Cathy, extending breath on the string of a kite

Part 4:
Knowing, Tradition, Release

Letter Sixteen:
Solitude

To You I Love,

Solitude has always been important to me, essential. I had my own room as a child, but now, as I gather years behind me, I am even more careful to place benches inside my heart, head, and gut on which to rest and reflect.

I like meeting you for shopping, museums, lunch, and walks, and I realize I also want to meet you at home, within. I want to know the richness there, the richness we share when we honor inner air with tables and chairs.

I sense a need for caution here, not wanting to invade.

You'll tell me what works for you, right?

And you know what that is, don't you?

Even though I said you are your own fairy godmother, I want to be a fairy godmother too, and wave my wand, and say:

"I give you the ability to know and care for your own wants and needs, whatever they may be."

I honor who you are, and what you want and need, and maybe sometimes our wants and needs will coincide, but whether they do, or not, we always meet, with room for you and me.

Waving my wand with respect,
Cathy, a modern fairy godmother who honors your gifts

Letter Seventeen:

Tradition

To You I Love,

I wonder if the mother-in-law represents vulnerability in the male, an Achilles heel. The daughter-in-law is made aware that the man she loves did not spring whole from the head of Zeus. Who knew on that first meeting that he had a family and came with traditions of his own, as do you?

And yet, the two of you, individually and as a couple, meet fresh and new, to examine and choose, and, in that, create and cultivate your own rituals and traditions. Even if you were raised in the same village, with the same religion and culture, together you look and determine what you believe and what feels right to discard and what to keep.

This awareness is a continuation of the individuation process which began when you were born, when you sat up, and crawled, when you were two and five, thirteen and sixteen, eighteen and twenty-one. Who are you now and what do you need?

There is a well-known story of newlyweds that says a great deal about the merging of two lives. The new husband watches his bride cut off the ends of the brisket or the ham, depending on which culture tells the story. Husband inquires politely why his wife is cutting off his favorite part of the meat. She says that's how her mother always did it. When she calls to ask her mother why she cuts off the ends of the meat, her mother says that's how grandma always did it. When grandma is asked why she does it, she says she cuts the ends off so the meat fits in the pan. Ah! It has nothing to do with health, hygiene, or taste. It has to do with the size of the pan, an ancestral pan, now enlarged for two.

Tradition can be unifying. It can be sacred, and practical. It can be irrelevant and out of date. Each couple decides what traditions, rituals, and ceremony to make their own, and it's important to keep something of the past. We are connected front and back. In that, we circle round and round, balancing on thermals like condors and hawks, as we navigate the hills and valleys that warm and cool the ground.

> Loving tradition, broken and caught,
> *Cathy,* both modern, and not

Letter Eighteen:
Tradition Re-Mixed

To You I Love,

Years ago, I was in Thailand and saw a Christmas ornament with Santa on the cross.

Then I heard a joke about the Easter Bunny pushing aside a stone and seeing his shadow. The world is a composite of beliefs, and sometimes they re-combine in new and creative ways.

Only you can know, select, and keep what traditions work for you.

When my sons were young, we read a book by J.R.R. Tolkien called *The Father Christmas Letters*. Tolkien didn't have much money in those days, so each year his children received a letter informing them of what went on that year at the North Pole. Father Christmas had an assistant, the North Polar Bear. Though he was a sweet and well-intentioned bear, he was clumsy, and his mishaps usually meant there weren't any gifts, but there was a letter explaining what had happened, and drawings too. No one could get angry at the North Polar Bear. After we read that book, amazingly enough, the North Polar Bear began writing a Christmas letter to my sons, commenting on events that occurred during that year, both at the Pole and in our household. One never knows when magic will enter and how tradition will unfold.

I look forward to seeing what emerges from the two of you. Be bold, and not. It is enough to know that strands, like tinsel, mirror.

> Knowing there are no mistakes,
> *Cathy,* tossing flakes of silver and gold

Letter Nineteen:
Perfection Release

To You I Love,

I wanted to be first in my husband's life, to be the best wife ever. Insane, we might say now, but it is what I thought I wanted, or maybe it is what I was trained to think I should want. I wanted a relationship unlike anything that had ever gone before. My standards were high, ridiculously, impossibly, and insanely high. I thought I could excel beyond the fairy tale ideal of living happily ever after. I would place my image of marriage up in the stars, spread galaxy-wide across the skies. You, daughters-in-law of today, already wiser than I, might perceive some problems, might see a supernova in the making.

My parents were excellent people, and I was raised in gentle trust. The bar was high for me to surpass, and yet I was determined to do just that, without knowing what that meant. My husband and I met, and we agreed. We would create the idealized nineteen fifties model to an extreme.

Of course there was a problem, one we didn't even know enough to know. We knew nothing about anger, fear, sadness, or good enough. We were raised to be happy, sunshine all the time. We had good lives, and in reality, when it comes to what is needed to survive and thrive, we had it all:

food, shelter, work, play, family, friends, and yet, there is a natural rhythm to life. The tides come in; the tides go out.

We have had to learn how to settle into a more natural rhythm, one less governed by mind over matter and absolutes, one more open to ups and downs, and ins and outs. That has not always been easy, and has sometimes been painful. We each have had to learn how to release kite strings of ego, to learn humility, surrender, receptivity, and letting go. We continue to learn to separate stimulus and response. Now, rather than immediately ripping the branch of anger off the tree, then, sharpening the end to a dagger's point and tossing it like a spear at the other, we try to hang out for a second, or two, and swing quietly from that branch for awhile, a short while. It is not helpful to go to bed angry. We know we need to talk. "When this happened, I thought this. I want. I need. My positive intention is that we find something that works for us both." We're still learning, but we both know that this idea of "perfection" allows no room for movement or growth. I wouldn't wish it on my worst enemy, and I certainly don't wish it on you.

I say, *"Perfection, sink back into the pond from which you rose. The poison apple is tied to a false idea of beauty as perfection. Let perfection take a bite of the poison apple that is itself, and die."*

> With love of release,
> *Cathy,* surrendered, some of the time

Letter Twenty:
Perfection Reframed

To You I Love,

When, seemingly out of the blue, the Dark Night of the Soul, also known as the mid-life crisis, hit my husband and me, we had no tools. We didn't know about shining a light on the shadow so it would disappear. We didn't know about shadow. We had no experience of therapy, and if we had, we would have considered it a stigma, failure, and weakness. Ask for help? No way! Stoic and stalwart, it was always noon in our lives, until it wasn't, and then finding the shadow, and allowing it, and learning from it was a process that took years, painful years, but years well-spent. After all, what else are we here to do?

    We had no idea what we were up against until we went to couples' therapy, and the first question asked concerned our vision of marriage. I went on and on about how nineteen fifties TV sitcoms like "Leave it to Beaver", "Father Knows Best", and "Donna Reed", had nothing on us. Except for the pearls and high heels, I was better than that. I knew what to do. Perfection was it. Steve nodded in agreement. I'm a little embarrassed to admit this now, and I can see you smiling sadly, but that is how we thought and felt, or thought we felt.

It wasn't until I heard Marion Rosen, founder of Rosen Method Bodywork and Movement, say, "Perfection is static," that I realized my goal had been a prison, and I had placed the bars. Perfection was not only unachievable, it wasn't even desirable. What was I trying to do? And there is another killer word, "try". Remember Yoda's admonition in the movie "Star Wars":*"Do or do not... there is no try."*

When I came to Rosen Method, part of the training was a week-long retreat. On our day off, we could paint. I didn't do art, learned at an early age that an artist I was not. Nevertheless I figured the beginning meditation was safe, and guided by Summer's voice, I walked through mist to sit on a rock behind a waterfall, a rock that overlooked a valley. Permission granted, I picked up a brush and painted my heart on silk, painted my heart like a kite, flying with other hearts like kites. And people saw my painting as art.

Now I paint on silk and frame my paintings in hoops, what I call sacred hoops. I balance flow and boundary knowing each of us is an artist. There are no rules or restrictions, and yet there is containment. An artist is like a baby looking out through the bars of a crib. The bars offer something to grip, a place to climb, and the rail is a place to hold onto and stand. I've changed the bars of my self-created prison to bars of a crib, a place where it's safe to explore and where I understand that like the sea we are rocked in the hands of land, and purpose knows both flow and probe.

> With intention to roll like a hoop,
> *Cathy,* who honors the muse as she bounds
> unbound from within

Part 5:
Today's Curve of the Tribe

Letter Twenty-One:
Women Today

To You I Love,

Things are changing, have always changed. As the kaleidoscope turns, patterns re-arrange, and re-arrange again. Today many people choose to marry later. They may choose their mate. They may marry someone of the same sex. Where I live, women are no longer property or slaves. It is time therefore to view the mother-in-law and daughter-in-law relationship with new eyes. We know about mirror neurons which may form a base for empathy, the social fluid. We know that touch releases what some call a love hormone. We are learning about social lubrication and how to communicate our wants and needs, which allows space for each of us and our beliefs.

Relationships between women have changed. They are friends and mentors. They play on the same sports teams and are represented equally at the Olympics. They work together and support each other. Emails circle around the internet about what women mean to each other. Relationships between women are honored and celebrated. Where would we be without our women friends?

Despite that, mother-in-law jokes continue. The entertainment industry encourages the myth of the judgmental, controlling mother-in-law who will not release her son. Who can respect a woman who won't release her son? Who can respect anyone who won't release? That's where wars begin, with an inability to accept the growth in change.

The image of a controlling mother sets up a dynamic in which the son may be caught in a push-pull between two women, both of whom he loves, and both of whom love him. The wife comes first. We all know that, and yet there is another who deserves honoring and respect. I know there are exceptions, and I note that the mother is not *owed* anything. She must earn respect. I think of the story of Solomon. Two women wanted the same child. To determine the mother, Solomon said he would cut the child in two. The real mother gave way. It is essential that the mother give way, honoring that there is a time to hold on, and a time to let go.

I don't know when divisiveness among women began, but I see nothing to be gained by it. Women have learned to integrate their parts, Madonna-whore, woman-child. They step on and off the pedestal. They work in a variety of ways. They learn to choose what nurtures them. They are able and expected to support themselves. They are aware, and awake, and in that, they bond.

Mark Twain said, "The secret source of humor itself is not joy but sorrow." Perhaps we really want to cry at these images that portray the mother-in-law with rancor and disgust. What do these images say about each of us? I wonder if disrespect of mother, any mother, leads to environmental pollution, as we then disrespect and dishonor Mother Earth.

I'm not trying to be a spoil-sport, and halt the spread of laughter which is so good for our health, but I don't think humor that separates us is what we want. We want to bond in our humanity, and our imperfection, but not at the expense of a group of people of which I am a part.

I believe we all benefit when we respect Mother, Mother-in-law, and Mother Earth. The word mother comes from the Latin, *mater, matter*. We all thrive when we respect the matter from which we are birthed.

> In appreciation of Mother, Mother Earth, and
>   humor that uplifts,
> *Cathy*, in love of change as it riffs

Letter Twenty-Two:
Such Wealth

To You I Love,

You now have a mother and a mother-in-law. You may have others who also fill that role. I wonder, "Where's my place?" and I don't always know. I do know that we may have more in common than might at first be obvious.

I don't know how many women I've heard say that they didn't realize how like their mother-in-law they were until she died. I was trekking in the Everest region of Nepal when my mother-in-law died. The people who live there believe all souls circle Everest before they depart. I felt my mother-in-law dip down for a hug, and wrap my heart like a scarf.

It was rarely possible for a woman of her generation to have the kind of freedom I had, but I know she would have loved to be there with me, and she was. I'm grateful I was in the mountains when she died. It freed and bonded us both. I would also have liked to have been here, with her, to have held her hand when she passed. I also missed being with my own mother at the moment of transition, though we spoke on the phone just moments before, and I felt a flutter of wings, a change in the air. I remember sitting with her when she was in Intensive Care, counting her breaths, savoring the preciousness of each one. I called them "miniature masterpieces" as I honored how she counted my first breaths, and steps, and I was counting her last.

We are learning to look at death differently, to offer letting go a safe landing. We are learning to release. We are also learning that competition and hierarchy in relationship are relics of the past. As Margaret Mead said, "Always remember that you are absolutely unique. Just like everyone else."

We live with abundance, and we love to give, and we do. There is enough for each of us to bond in our uniqueness, just like everyone else.

There is room.

> Unique,
> *Cathy,* softly landing a pace

Letter Twenty-Three:
Play with Blocks

To You I Love,

Okay you say, this is all great and good, but there are times when you, meaning me, are challenging. Yes, I hear you. I honor ebb and flow, and I know, that, yes, even I may have my moments, and now it's time to think about that, and smile.

Smiling is a gift. It releases all kinds of spirits and joy. We hear a smile over the phone. I like to envision the backs of my knees in a smile, my belly, my heart. Sometimes the smile is subtle and sly, and other times it erupts in laughter raucous and loud, but it always feels good to smile.

Smiling helps us re-frame, changes how we see this moment, this moment, now. With a smile, I can put myself in the shoes, moccasins or bare feet of another. I can be the child who when asked why roses have thorns, replied "So fairies have a place to hang their wings when they swim!"

In 1946, Viktor Frankl wrote *Man's Search for Meaning*, a book about how he survived a concentration camp in Nazi Germany during WWII. He wrote: "When we are no longer able to change a situation...We are challenged to change ourselves."

In the game of Scrabble, we pick little squares and place

them on the board for points. Okay, that's a game, but this is a game too. We are given parameters, within which to work, play, and respond. I hope no one ever again is confronted with what Viktor Frankl went through, but I wonder if we can remember our kaleidoscope and create new patterns of response as we turn it round and round.

> With intention to be as easy as pie,
> *Cathy,* who knows that making a pie is not
>   a piece of cake

Letter Twenty-Four:
Acceptance

To You I Love,

Charlotte Selver, the founder of Sensory Awareness, was a great teacher for me. I met her when I was forty-four, and continue to learn from her, and hear her voice in my head, though she died in 2003 at the age of 102. I use her words to soften the edges I meet. She and Marion Rosen, another teacher I revere, and the founder of Rosen Method, survived Nazi Germany by seeing what was coming and fleeing to the United States. Both missed Germany at times, because it was their home, the place of their birth. It is clear to me that Charlotte and Marion lived the substance of these words.

> *Life does not flow in any particular way.*
> *But in the moment that I can accept*

that it doesn't flow always the way I want,
I can allow gradually, a little more
the possibility, to meet it as it is.
Then, perhaps, through this allowing,
conditions change.

—Charlotte Selver

With intention to honor the gifts of my teachers,
Cathy, a student til death do me part, and, even then ...

Letter Twenty-Five:
Value of the Tribe

To You I Love,

In the past, women worked together to gather berries, tend fires, raise children, and cook. Gender roles were clear. The worst punishment was banishment from the tribe because survival was unlikely. It may be less obvious to those of us who feign independence, but we still need a tribe. We are social creatures, and even the introverts among us, are social beings. Look at the worlds within, the microorganisms and organizations of cells into liver, stomach, heart.

Driving home one day, I heard a siren and saw flashing lights. I pulled over to the side of the road as an ambulance raced by, surprised when tears filled my eyes. I hoped that someone was saved, but no matter what, I appreciated the effort that the ambulance represents, the intention our community sets to honor and save one life. We unite in our belief in the value and worth of each member of the tribe. We cannot survive on our own. We share one planet, one ship.

When my seventeen-year-old niece was diagnosed with a serious disease, her treatment required huge numbers of dedicated people. It was another example of how we, as a society, care. We unite to save a life, and each of us, unites daily in sharing the fullness of life. Our morning coffee involves a huge inter-connectedness, even as our evening meal orients and aligns.

We are brought together as members of a tribe, of many tribes. It's exciting to share our lives, and know we are parts of an ever-evolving and rapidly changing whole. I don't know how long I will be here, but I do know that each moment is a gift.

> Grateful to share a tepee, a tribe, a planet, a ship,
> *Cathy*, who appreciates how we connect

Part 6:
Artistry

Letter Twenty-Six:
Lifting the Veil

To You I Love,

I read somewhere that you can uncover what is meaningful for you when you remember back to what you thought about when you sat on the toilet when you were nine or ten. What sparked for you at that age?

I loved to read and ride my bike, and swing on my swing set. I'd pump my legs, lean back and brush my feet against the sky. It was my way to paint. I loved to daydream, and slip head first down a slide like an otter in snow.

Silence was a given in my childhood, time for silence. My father built a boat and I would sit on the front of the boat as we moved along the water, immersed in my own thoughts, or perhaps in all thought. We loved to camp. My father placed potatoes in the embers of the fire to roast. I remember us sitting together looking up at stars.

We didn't talk about silence. We just were.

I raise the veil on silence now, let it out, reveling in vibration, not yet known as sound.

Can we lift the veil on words, and see the face of silence unveiled?

Can we listen inside?
What reverberates when we pause?
How many veils shimmer? Are we open to meet the muse?

> Living a'mused,
> *Cathy,* veiled and unveiled, depending on mood

Letter Twenty-Seven:
Authenticity

To You I Love,

Sometimes I think the mother-in-law and daughter-in-law should create a ritual, devise some sort of vow, and then, I think how much I don't like pressure to bond. The whole point of what I'm saying is that I don't want there to be pressure between us, no pressure to be silent, share, or talk. I want us to rise and fall in a natural rhythm like jellyfish in the sea.

Years ago, I participated in a Woman's Challenge class. We climbed up cliffs, helped each other across crevasses, and used ropes to rappel each other down. The idea was to put ourselves in dangerous situations, so we would bond enough on one three-day weekend to become life-long friends. I found it artificial. My barriers went up. Nobody tells me when and how to bond. Friendship is not a given. It is a gift, a grace-filled gift, which sometimes requires intention, flexibility, resilience, and work.

That said, now that I'm older and hopefully softened and less ego-driven by proclamations of independence, I find myself considering what two women of different generations might write or say to proclaim their union, connection, bond. I offer these words, recognizing you may have your own words, or not, and all of it is okay. We're here in trust, in love with imagination and artistry. Remember the treasure chest, full, when empty. This is only a suggestion I offer to you.

Dearly Beloved, we are gathered here together. Two women of different generations and backgrounds meet here, two women who love, honor, and respect the same man, and who know this man differently. One knows the boy, and parts of the man, perhaps in a brackish way, that mix of salt water and fresh, while the other knows the mature man, and the little boy, so, again, a mix, and here we are, each with a cauldron of creativity. How do we meet, mix, merge, separate, and honor the alchemical process again and again?

We know the moon affects the tides. We bleed monthly, until we don't, and yet, we continue to know and honor cycles. We circle and release. We don't need a ring exchange because the earth rises in us, like sap in trees. We live open and closed, empty and full, dancing and still, as daughters of the moon.

We know how to reflect. We are artists in how we live. We create ritual and tradition and let it go, again and again. We honor meeting new, and changing mood. We honor we are two.

<blockquote>
Reflecting,
Cathy, settling ease
</blockquote>

Letter Twenty-Eight:
One of My Ways

To You I Love,

Angeles Arrien, a cross-cultural anthropologist, invites us to answer three questions devised by the philosopher Baruch Spinoza (1632-1677) and, through our answers, to change our life. A friend and I have been doing just that.

We began with the three Spinoza questions, emailing our answers to each other before we went to bed. Then, they weren't enough to express the fullness of our day as it was now expanding outward and inward with our increased observation and appreciation, so we added five more. Now, I answer them throughout the day, then, email my reflections at night.

I offer the questions as invitations, the first three from Spinoza, via Angeles Arrien, and the last five our continuing examination and exploration.

1. *Who or what inspired me today?*
2. *Where have I experienced peace, comfort, balance or satisfaction today?*
3. *What made me happy today that was not relationally dependent? Only I am responsible for my happiness.*

4. *What made me joyous today? How did joy enhance my day?*
5. *When was I creative today? How creative am I in my definition of creativity?*
6. *What am I grateful for?*
7. *How did I love today?*
8. *How and when did I connect, with myself, with the environment, and with others?*

I know you're wondering if something so simple really works. About three months after we began, I was at a holiday party, and someone commented on how happy I looked, and asked me why. People gathered round, and asked, "Yes, you do look happy. Why?" Now, that in itself is a little odd considering how beautiful it is where I live, and how those at the party, and I, have more than enough to eat and be and do, but I thought about it, and realized, "It's the Spinoza questions," and I began to explain and share.

I also expounded on my intention to be creative with and nourish inner air. I play with breath, tunnel and build castles and fairy houses, and connect them with tiny forest paths, wind-blown dunes, and super highways. I inhale, both curious and grateful, and exhale, wondering how far breath goes and how it is shared. I play with the leaves of plants, touch and tickle, aware that plants and I are tied. We are dependent on each other in our carbon dioxide-oxygen exchange.

Do I do this all the time? No, obviously not, but I do have intention for it. Answering the questions means I pause before bed. I pause to remember and reflect, to honor what is given, received, and exchanged that day. It may be from leaves, trees, people, land, stones, and sea.

It may be a cliché to say we create our world, but I believe we do. I believe when we live as artists, honoring how we breathe and perceive, we augment and expand the gifts in a day. This is my belief. It may not be yours. We each have our ways.

Johannes Itten writes in *The Art of Color* that: "Any two colors that are not precisely complementary will tend to shift the other towards its own complement ... both will lose their intrinsic character and move in an individual field or action of an unreal kind, as if in a new direction."

Now what do we make of that?

>   Inspiration, balance, happiness, joy, creativity, gratitude, love, and connection,
>   *Cathy,* with intention to complement and compliment exchange

Letter Twenty-Nine:
Art of Love

To You I Love,

Van Gogh wrote, "The more I think it over, the more I feel that there is nothing more artistic than to love people."

As I've said, I got the message in school that I wasn't artistic. Now, I read the words of Van Gogh and, inspired, unfold the canvas of my heart, and draw, paint, and sculpt. I twine my hands in prayer, and sometimes make a steeple. Then, I turn my fingers up and marvel at all the people.

Well, now, I hear you say, that's a game you play, imaginative, true, but it's not always so easy to love people. It's not like everyone is easy to love. That's true. Not everyone is easy to love, and where might we begin? Who might be really tough to love? Might we begin with loving ourselves? Ouch! Sometimes, that's tough. We may have been taught not to brag, to be modest and humble, a silent, conscientious member of the tribe. My generation of women was taught to keep our legs together and white gloves clean. It took time for me to learn to be my own cheerleader. I still struggle with it, but once in awhile, I can raise a pompom in each hand and jump in the air and give a shout, a shout for myself. Sometimes I envision a waterfall of those moments, prisms for the sun, forming rainbows caught in well-placed pots of gold.

Recently a woman said to me that I must be a dancer. My first response was, "Oh, no, my mother was a dancer. She took ballet as a child, was lithe and limber and light and tossed through the air and hated it, so I never had dance lessons, so I am not a dancer." And then I caught myself. Of course I am a dancer. We all are. Every movement is dance. My arms are branches. My feet have roots that move the earth. My arms sweep the sky. My rib cage loves to prance. I am a dancer.

> *I cheerlead myself.*
>
> *I am the lens through which I look.*
>
> *I soften the lens through which I look, and the world softens too.*
>
> *I fasten the diamond of each moment with prongs that adjust.*
>
> *I am Love; I am Life; I am Art. I am.*

Fulfilling and Fulfilled,
Cathy, an artist danced with Love

Letter Thirty:
Life as Hour-Glass

To You I Love,

One day, many years ago, I was leaning over the side of my deck feeling depressed when I felt a shift, as though I was held in the center, embraced at the waist. I was an hourglass. I realized I could hold myself centered, focused in the middle, and in that place, turn one way, and then the other. I was given a tool, an image I could use to balance my mood. I could choose the direction of flow, and keep the sand moving at my own pace. I had choice.

I learned at the same time that depression is anger directed at ourselves. I wondered why I would direct anger at myself. I'm not minimizing depression. I understand it can be uncontrollable for some, and outside help and medication may be needed, but I was not there.

I knew I wanted to create and cultivate a kit of tools, to find and nourish images of support for myself when I felt down. I began with loving myself. Remember the mirror? I look at myself in the mirror with eyes of kindness. Sometimes I put branches and roots on my hourglass and send anger and fear out my branches like flame. I wing my roots. I empower on what I envision. I also understand there is a place to honor grief. I'm creative there too. I become a swan and carry grief as she carries her babies, her cygnets, tucked into her feathers, on her back. Other times I give grief like bread crumbs to the geese.

Ruth Denison, a woman I admire and respect, a woman raped so many times by every side in Nazi Germany during WWII that she could never have children, said that when she was a child, her father told her to listen to the grass growing. Perhaps that is how she kept her innocence and dealt with such pain. She listened to the grass growing. I listen, too, and I listen to and talk to trees and leaves.

I know life will bring you pain, and though I would like to prevent it, I also know that's how you grow. Carl Perkins said, "If it weren't for the rocks in its bed, the stream would have no song." The artist in me sees the artist in you, sees your song ripple with light, as you dance your steps like pebbles skimmed on the sea. I want the best for you, the best of ease, trust, and knowing my care. I want you to know my care. I rest there.

> With intention to meet the bounce in streams,
> *Cathy,* honoring harvest in heart

Part 7:
A Caress You Inspire

Letter Thirty-One:
Donkey Time

To You I Love,

It may be obvious that I love to slow time, to pause, and reflect. Once in Nepal, in the mountains near Tibet, I spent an entire day watching a stream rush downhill. I still nourish on that stream, almost twenty years later. The book *The Wisdom of Donkeys, Finding Tranquility in a Chaotic World,* by Andy Merrifield, offers guidance that works for me. He writes "Time slows down among donkeys." I slow with those words, envision myself with a donkey, just sitting there stroking long ears. Merrifield quotes Milan Kundera who writes in his novel *Slowness*, that "Our society wants to blow out the tiny trembling flame of memory."

You and I may not have easy access to a donkey, but we do have tools, skills. We can visualize ourselves with a donkey or by a stream. We can kindle the "tiny trembling flame of memory" by slowing, and listening to ourselves, and to others, and to the creatures in the soil, and resting on the earth.

If time is about motion, then, stillness extends it. Slow down. Fairy tales of the past began with the words, "Once upon a time." We can unsaddle the word "once" and remove the harness. What works for us now?

Alan Watts wrote, "People in a hurry cannot feel." Yet, I believe we are here to feel, to wiggle around until we touch that place inside where joy and sorrow meet as one. I may be unusual, but, for me, the days and nights seem to lengthen with each year because I value them more and more. I stretch them on a long line of enthusiasm, appreciation, and joy. It may look like I'm sitting still, but stillness steps with donkey steps. I am content. And no matter what, I'm moving because I live on a planet that spins in space, in a galaxy that's spiral.

> In praise of slowing down,
> *Cathy,* who extends with stillness

Letter Thirty-Two:

Pain

To You I Love,

I want to protect you from pain. You want to protect me from pain. We protect each other. I was grateful I got breast cancer after my mother died, because I don't think she could have stood to see me suffer. It's painful to watch those we love suffer.

We make it through, though, don't we? We make it through pain. Our heart breaks open, and heals, again and again. We melt like ice, part like rock, become spacious and open to air, and close again. When I went through treatment for breast cancer, I learned I had value within my tribe. I learned my task was to receive, which is not as simple as it might seem. I had to learn to receive, to learn I completed a circuit and gave to others when I received.

I learned to see pain as a symphony. I would assign each area of pain a part, the rash, the scar, the gut, the heart, and let the pain play in me as the rasp of a stick across a board, a drum, a triangle, cymbal, cello, violin, and harp. One day I heard jackhammers as Tibetan bells. I didn't plan it. It's what I heard, and then, I saw the jackhammers. Oh, jackhammers, not bells. I received the lesson. I can choose how and what I perceive.

In treatment, I was vulnerable, dependent on others. I learned I couldn't judge in the way I had before. Chemotherapy, a poison, was ingested, to make me well. Black and white combined to make gray, to heal.

Brené Brown in a Ted Talk on "The Power of Vulnerability" says, "Connection is why we are here. We need the willingness to say 'I love you' first, the willingness to do things when there are no guarantees." Can I say, "I love you," to hurt and pain? Can I plant healing in the holes pain creates? It is my intent.

Brené Brown says that children are hard-wired for struggle and we should tell them that.

Though I doubt you consider yourself a child, I will say it anyway, because it isn't easy to realize children have grown up. "You are hard-wired for struggle." We are hard-wired for struggle, and we are hard-wired for glory. Reaching, we're reached. Vulnerable, we touch and connect.

> Embracing, embraced,
> *Cathy,* with holes for healing I plant with care

Letter Thirty-Three:

Forgiveness

To You I Love,

For years, I wore a sticker on the inside of my shoes, "Forgiveness is every step." I admire those who are able to forgive. My friend Etta B. Ehrlich writes that "Each time you judge yourself you break your own heart." We need to forgive for our health and the health of the world.

    I believe we each know of Anne Frank and her powerful diaries, but I only recently learned of Etty Hillesum, who died in Auschwitz in 1943. Though she was only twenty-nine, when she died, she had learned to find support within. She wrote: "All landscapes are within me and there is room for everything." Grief and pain passed through her and the peace she found reflected out toward others. I want to be like Etty, to reflect peace into the world. It is my goal.

    Elsa Gindler, the founder of a study of consciousness based on direct perception and now called Sensory Awareness, saved lives in Nazi Germany by teaching people to respond calmly when the SS demanded to know if they were Jewish. She would ask her students to make a fist, to make it as tight as they could. She would then say, "Feel what it does to you. How does it affect you, anywhere through you? Gradually let go of the fist and feel what's happening." This ability to feel what making a fist does to us and then let it go, may allow us to find another way to meet what happens in our lives. I want this for myself. I don't think I could ever have the courage of Elsa Gindler, who risked her life to teach, lead, and save, but I set intention for a small piece of what she was able to do.

Recently, as part of a sensing experiment, I lay on the floor with a stone the size of my fist on my chest. The stone felt light at first, and then, it felt heavy, and I felt myself meeting the stone, or the stone meeting me, and there was reverberation in my chest, rib cage to rib cage, and sky to ground. Something let go, some defense, and I felt I could meet myself and others more openly. I could begin, perhaps, slowly, gently, tenderly, to begin to make room for more.

I thought of the words of E.M. Forster in *Howard's End*: "Only Connect!"

I wondered if I could allow pain to rest, like a baby bird in a nest. Then I remembered baby birds squawk, so perhaps it is to let pain fly, and in that flight, begin to make a little more room for all that is singing, high and low, bitter and tragic, uplifting and sweet.

Thich Nhat Hanh, a Vietnamese Buddhist monk who was exiled from his home, Vietnam, because of his work for peace writes, "Our own life is the instrument with which we experiment with the truth." May I beckon the truth from within, inspired to relate.

With intention to be the change I want to see in the world, *Cathy,* with intention to receive and release

Letter Thirty-Four:

Permission

To You I Love,

Our homework one night during an *Eyes of the Beholder* workshop was to give ourselves an hour to do whatever we wanted to do. We were invited to feel our way into enchantment. I set the timer. One hour just to be present with me. I went outside and gathered and brought in wood and made a fire in the fireplace. I lit candles. I watched the flame. After awhile, I felt an inner stir, a need for a little more. I allowed an impulse to form and rose to make soup. I cut up vegetables and sautéed, added stock, opened a bottle of red wine, and sat by the fire. Hours passed.

When I told my son, he was shocked, and exclaimed, "You needed to pay someone to give you permission to rest?" I said, "Yes," and maybe times have changed, but from what I read, hear, and see, women are still driven to perform, and do, give, and care, and that is great, absolutely great, and sometimes we need to pause, go within, and renew.

Some mornings I go alone to the Dipsea Café, and order coffee and a veggie scramble. I sit quietly in the back by the fire, just sit, and often, tears come. I don't know why, just tears. I think of the words of Albert Camus, "Live to the point of tears." Sometimes, I do. William Blake said, "The deeper the sorrow, the greater the joy." I know that, too.

Each day, I set intention to allow myself a pause, a pause to feel. Is my cauldron empty or full, bubbling or stagnant? What is happening with me, in me, right now? Sometimes I write down what is happening because I have read that writing in a journal, even two minutes a day, can lift a mood.

I often pause to look at the moon. I stand outside on the days when I know it's full and watch its sunset rise. If I wake early enough, I can also see it set. I name each full moon. There is Vision Moon and Renewal Moon, Inner Moon and Outer Moon. Depending on its phase, I see it in the sky in day, and stand under it at night. I open my arms as wide as I possibly can, embraced. It is amazing this moon of ours, rhythmic in its accounting, and offering in its daily changes, permission to change our brew.

I, too, am full and new, light and dark, receiving light and passing it on, and not. I honor the moon in me, the moon in you. I am grateful for the weight of its presence, for its push and pull on the tides, in me, in you. I offer my ways of invitation and permission to you, and wait here open, to receive what bubbles, brews, and reflects in you.

> An admirer of the change in light,
> *Cathy,* inviting gravitational play

Letter Thirty-Five:
Communion

To You I Love,

We are each a composite, a balancing act of male and female, doing and being, external and internal.

We honor both masculine and feminine, in ourselves, and in each other.

We recognize stillness and action. We give and receive.

We know the movement of air. We feel the movement of air in and out. We feel the wind, and sniff the breeze.

We can be the boat; we can be the sea. We can be the paddle that once was tree.

And we can pause.

These letters are meant to open a dialogue.

In Sensory Awareness, we say we "come to standing" or "come to sitting" or "come to lying". It is how we honor the journey, remind ourselves that we can be aware and notice all along the way. I'm still working with this, being with myself all along the way. For me, it is a means of communion, a way of knowing and coming home, a home that expands with age. I give thanks for communion, for breaking silence with another with the same honoring as I break bread, for knowing the union that comes when I am present with the gift of myself, and others, all along the way.

My intention with these letters is to come in and out of communion with you. We open and close, aware, awake.

> With intention,
> *Cathy*, allowing space

Part 8:
Threshold

Letter Thirty-Six:
Receiving

To You with Whom I Circle,

I was in a circle one day, again with *Eyes of the Beholder,* and everyone was sharing how much they give. Finally, someone asked, "With all this giving, who is receiving?" We all sat stunned. Surely, there wasn't another circle of people saying, "I just keep receiving and receiving. I don't know how to stop." That made no sense. The center of our circle felt like a Black Hole, sucking and sucking, a gravitational field of no escape. Giving and receiving is a circle of energy. We have two hands. We use both. We pass the rope of life through both hands to give, pause, and receive.

There is a song "Magic Penny" by Malvina Reynolds, "Love is something if you give it away, give it away, give it away, you end up having more." No one could argue with that, and yet, we also need to receive, to bow in humility and accept gifts, banquet loads of gifts. It is part of the cycle of life and death.

I know it feels vulnerable to receive. We worry we'll be perceived as needy or weak. Maybe we'll be dumped from the tribe, be seen as greedy or selfish, or not a worthy and perpetually giving part of the team. I had to learn to receive when I was undergoing chemotherapy and radiation. In that, I learned how much people want to give. We want to give, and we learn to receive.

I think of these letters as doors, windows. Some windows may be stained, wounds. We've been walking from room to room, each letter an invitation. Now I offer room for you to reflect and tell me what you need, or not. This invitation is for you, in honor of you, in full taste and embrace of what we share.

> Head bowed,
> *Cathy*, open in invitation

Letter Thirty-Seven:
A Moving View

To You I Love,

I write this looking out on a redwood tree that began as one and rises as two. There is also an oak, ripe with new growth. Baby trees sprout at their feet.

   One June I was on a cruise ship savoring where water meets land in Alaska and British Columbia. I was entranced with a movable view. Hour after hour, day after day, I sat, stood and walked, looking and receiving, looking for whales and dolphins, watching the sun rise, and set, tracking the phases of the moon. Life was defined on the ship, or so I thought. I knew its boundary and felt artificially safe. I was surprised to love it so much. I have a tendency toward claustrophobia. What was different? My moving view, I thought, and then, one day, I realized I always have a moving view. I live on a ship, circling, turning, moving through space and giving me new views of sun, moon, and stars. How do I forget? How do I forget to greet each moment with awareness, with beginner's mind, to remember I live as kaleidoscope, turning, and meeting new ways to greet and shape the light.

Trees change before my eyes, grow and reproduce. Can I see?

Sometimes, I do.

And now I ask, "What moves you?"

And again, this is for you, not me, no need to respond, no want or need, no push or desire.

> Beaming like a lighthouse,
> *Cathy,* turning with land and sea

Letter Thirty-Eight:
Answer the Request

To You I Love,

My teacher of Sensory Awareness, Charlotte Selver, used to say that people spend time in the beginning of things and in the middle of things but avoid the endings. She was emphatic on emphasizing that every moment of this journey we are on the way. She would ask us to lift our arm, and notice all along the way. We would come to standing over and over again, noticing along the way.

It's fun to be "on the way," and maybe that's why it's fun to be on a ship. It's clear we are moving, but, as I've said, we are on a ship, this beautiful planet Earth. Charlotte would emphasize over and over again that "Every moment has a certain request on us. The question is how we answer it."

How do we answer the request? Steve Jobs answered his last moment with, *"Oh, Wow. Oh, Wow, Oh, Wow."* I want to answer each moment with, "Oh, Wow!" I had a dream where I opened a manhole cover, and looked out on a vast, flat, bare landscape. I saw the empty expanse as an invitation to set my course and quest. I felt exhilaration in my chest.

One day, I hiked with a friend to a stream. We sat on rocks and watched the water pour and pool. A frog sat with us, a sentry. We had each lost our fathers when we were young, and we came to enjoy, but also to honor and grieve. Then, something rippled through the water, and we felt we were not alone. I wonder now if the frog was a prince sharing his amphibious nature. The frog lives on water and land. Perhaps he also navigates between the living and the dead. I read somewhere that the Zuni say, "The distance between the living and the dead is thinner than a strand of hair." That day, we thrilled to the whip of a horse hair worm parting the liquid that stirred.

The notes of music need silence. Perhaps, we do too.

> Believing that a frog can guide and transform without even a kiss,
> *Cathy,* who writes her tales to answer request

Letter Thirty-Nine:
Conclusion as Threshold

To You I Love,

Why did I write these letters to you?

I thought I wanted to look at the mother-in-law and daughter-in-law relationship, and I did, and I do, but now, I know I also wanted to thank those women who've given such meaning and teaching to my life, those women who've now passed. I wanted to apologize for not listening more closely, for not being more receptive, for not opening and expanding the stone of myself, so I could bring the water in the well a little closer to the bucket from which we all drink. These letters, this book is my thank you to these women, to all women, to all we share. They are, of course, also, to you, and to me.

Albert Einstein suggested that we each come to see that we inhabit a world much larger than we realize. I think we are like the chick in the egg, tiny at first, and then, we grow bigger and bigger, until we burst out into a world with other chicks and trees, and we keep doing that, exclaiming, "Oh, wow," over and over again.

I might have listened more. I listen now. We are beads on a chain, a chain that goes back to the beginning. We can use the chain to jump the rope of being, to open, close, and explore. We can use it to connect and release.

My son carried you over a threshold. We carry ourselves over threshold after threshold. We meet ourselves, and we meet each other. We grow and claim. The cauldron is full now as our brew turns to a nurturing stew guided by the phases of the moon.

                        Gratefully Blessed,
                        Cathy, releasing the reins

Letter Forty:
Bringing in My Sons

To You I Love,

My sons and I read many books together, *Wind in the Willows, Winnie the Pooh, The Old Man and the Sea,* but one stands out right now, the story, *Moths and Mothers, Feathers and Fathers, A Story about a Tiny Owl Named SQUIB.* It was lovingly written and illustrated by Larry Shles. Squib's father would toss tiny owl Squib from tuft to tuft, from ear to ear, and Squib would slide down into his father's soft feathered head.

I open that book now, and see a note I wrote who knows how many years ago, *"To my Little Squiblet, A sweet, loving story. Love, Mom."* Four *x*'s and four *o*'s prance across the page, with the words, *"I love you, Squiblet!"* and so it goes. This feeling of love is unbounded, essential, renewing and strong, like that continuing cycle of moisture flowing through us, clouds, and trees. It's all we need.

This is the fortieth letter, honoring the words, as I said in the beginning, of Jelaluddin Rumi, "What nine months does for the embryo, forty early mornings will do for your growing awareness."

I don't know if you will read these letters in the morning or at night, or at all, but my wave of a wand wish is that these forty letters may offer nourishment and strength to assist you in your tasks, and the fulfillment of your every quest. My heart is with you, ringed and shared. You are my *belle-fille*. I may be your *belle-mere*. We are both beautiful, graced in all we share.

In Love, I Trust

Each breath we share, a parachute,

    dropping us deeply forward and inward

  with gentleness and care.

From loving tuft to loving tuft,
Cathy, also known as *"Mom", "Mother-in-law",* and *"Mother-in-love"*

Epilogue:

Years ago, my mother gave me a tiny card with four pink hearts one on top of the other. Today, I see them as a lighthouse of hearts, which brings me to the words of Anne Lamott, "Lighthouses don't go running all over an island looking for boats to save; they just stand there shining."

My intention with these letters is to be a lighthouse, standing here shining. My wave of the wand wish is that we stack light with those we love, and enter each harbor safely, knowing all travel and journey as home.

Acknowledgments

I want to express my gratitude and thanks to women - mother, grandmothers, mother-in-law, daughters-in-law, niece, sisters-in-law, family, teachers, and friends. I express my thanks to men - father, husband, sons, brother, family, teachers, and friends.

It's challenging to single out, but Karen Roeper and Jane Flint led Eyes of the Beholder which I mention many times here, and Elaine Chan-Scherer and I met when she was having surgery on her brain and I was beginning chemotherapy. She has two daughters and because she had such an amazing relationship with her mother-in-law wants this for them. My niece Katy is my jewel, and, of course, Jan and Frieda, these letters are for you. I know we meet as streams, each flowing and unique, joined as one in ocean tides of thought, love and care.

Thanks also to Mudita Nisker, Dan Clurman, Mahdiah Esther Jacobs Kahn, Susan Adelle, Amrita Blaine, Ellen Sennewald, Sara Gordon, and all my family and friends and more people than I ever need to count because I know we all are one. Angeles Arrien has been an inspiration through my many friends who have studied with her. I thank her for her books and for what friends have shared with me from their work with her. Thanks, of course, to Charlotte Selver and Marion Rosen.

Thanks especially to Jeff and Chris and Steve. Without these three, I can't imagine where I would be. They are my guides. They are my lights, and they turn my kaleidoscope in ways and dimensions I could never conceive on my own. I am blessed and grateful to have them in my life.

Daughters-in-Love

The end and the beginning
A spiral organizing inside out
Passage, birth, letting go
I know myself through you
Perhaps you know yourself through me
Maiden, woman, crone, warriors of the moon,
Stirrers of a cauldron,
Guidance of the rune.

www.ingramcontent.com/pod-product-compliance
Lightning Source LLC
Chambersburg PA
CBHW072056290426
44110CB00014B/1707